Xavier Wakes

by Michael Soper

Saint Francis Xavier
7 April 1506 - 3 December 1552

"MAIOR IN OCCASU"
Greater in Death

Given to the world, in God's eternal reign,
To win for God much of the world again.
Camoes, *The Lusiads,* Canto One, 6

Other books by Michael Soper

Stepping Stones
Reversed
Decrypted
What Happens After You Flunk French?
Impressions
Confessions
100 Exceptional English-language Poems
Something About Mary
Dead Poets

ISBN-10: 1479355046

ISBN-13: 978-1479355044

Copyright Registration: TX 7-554-079

Invocation

from the Red Chapel in Czechoslovakia,
a prayer to Saint Frantisek Xaversky

You left your home to preach The Word,
and served your life beyond the seas.
Rejoicing in the love of Christ,
you brought the heathen to their knees.

At last, they came to know God's love,
and how our Savior set them free.
Their souls abide with you above,
and with the One who is the Three.

Oh Xavier, hear my prayer !
I am a poor sinner too:
Help me to endure my grief,
and keep me in God's love with you.

Introduction

When Francis Xavier left Lisbon for Portuguese India, he was accompanied by the Governor, endowed by the King, and commissioned by the Pope. He was charged by the first Jesuits to set the world on fire. It's hard to imagine how he could have exceeded his authority, but he did. Walking from village to village, sailing from island to island, and baptizing the native inhabitants by the thousand, he created defenseless minority communities. Teaching them the articles of Christian faith in their own tongues, he set up the charges that would later be used against his Order: blasphemy, heresy. Xavier, unintentionally, set the stage for intrigue and slaughter. So did the Apostles.

The criticism that seems to stick, is that Xavier left his post. Though he always returned to Goa, he was always leaving, for Ceylon, Malacca, Japan, or rushing to the rescue of one of his native Christian enclaves. He was expected to administer the Church in Portuguese India, to recruit and train and build, to correspond, to administer its funds, to tame its soldier-sailors, and to serve as Father Confessor to the elite of the colony. But he did. The surviving "Letters and Instructions of Francis Xavier" are, mostly, instructions. To paraphrase them all, he would say, send this

one, recall that one, receive these two and train
them, disburse certain funds as follows, visit
this one or that one and remind him of his
promise or his obligation, expand this, abandon
that, or, impossibly, and each time too late,
Come! Quickly! He would tell his subordinates
to read his instructions twice, to obey them, to
reply twice by different ships to acknowledge
each order and to report each task complete.
And then, he told them that he loved them.

Xavier is remembered, and beloved, for his
missionary letters, not for his administrative
instructions. These letters have inspired
generations of missionaries to follow.
And for his letters, Francis Xavier is the Patron
Saint of the Propagation of the Faith. If he
expected too much of his Brothers in Christ,
excuse him. He worked himself to death in ten
years. He died, marooned on a tiny island, with
his second and first objectives in sight, China
and Heaven.

Word of his betrayal and death spread, and
other Portuguese, his friends, returned for his
bones. They found, instead, Xavier's body, so
fresh that it could still bleed.
They brought him back to Goa, and placed him
in a glass casket in front of the altar, where this
book begins.

Michael T. Soper

Return to Goa

March 1554, the uncorrupted body of
Francis Xavier is returned to Goa, India.

Do not, O Sacred Guardian, hide your face
From those whose only harbor is your grace!
Camoes, *The Lusiads,* Canto Two, 31

I am carried in a great procession,
through torch-lit streets, from the ship
to the chapel in the College of St. Paul.
For days and nights the people pass
    the open casket
and stare, or weep, or wonder, or pray.
Someone remembers and brings children
    to sing.
And the story is already told,
how the devout Captain Aragao,
how my devoted friend Joam Beira,
sailed to Sancian and to Malacca
to recover my remains.
I would have prevented the risk
-- even to the ships.

But to risk a crew for a corpse?
Not for the Twelve Apostles.
I returned in the usual stages, as freight.
For their reverence, I forgive the crews
the disturbance and their morbid curiosity.
Contemplation, through me, of their own
    mortality

improved them, as sailors and Christians,
as fathers and sons. Therefore,
I am content to be on display.
But let this be my final resting place.
If Goa gives offense to God, I will burn
    it down.
But if you bring your unbearable burden to me,
and repent your sins, and love God,
then I will ease your inconsolable grief.
I will give you Peace.

Green Bay Wisconsin

Death of Ignatius

31 July 1556, Ignatius of Loyola is dying.

". . . reverend Father of my soul . . . recommend me to
God . . . in your . . . prayers, so that . . . after this
restless life will have ended, he may reunite us. . . "
Xavier to Ignatius, 1549

With recharged spirit he ordered the bo'sun
To spread all sails and head for the ocean.
Camoes, The Lusiads, Canto Two, 64

Here you are, so very old, so much the same.
I followed the prayers raised in your name.
It is Francisco, my spirit, your worthless
   servant.
Though you save my soul, I cannot save
   your life.
I have always thought that we would be
with family in Spain, with friends in Paris,
with brothers in Rome, with saints in
   Jerusalem,
with Jesus in Heaven. We would be together.
But somehow, I am bound to Earth,
and you are finally free, and now,
for the greater glory of God,
you sail the Galaxy.

The Storm

Cochin India, 1557, at a canonical investigation
into the life of Francis Xavier, a wandering
sea captain testifies.

The black clouds dispersed and a resonant
Moaning echoed over the sea.
    Camoes, *The Lusiads*, Canto Five, 60

Xavier sailed from Cochin
aboard my ship before.
But he was dead, or he is not dead
according to some lore.
We set sail on Good Friday,
though we could have stayed in port,
and Easter is a holy time,
but all my time is short.
I gave an extra offering,
I thought it would suffice.
We sailed for southern islands
with cloth to trade for spice.

And we were, every one of us,
decent Christian men.
We knew each other's vices,
forgave each other's sin.
The cook took bigger portions,
as if we couldn't tell.
The steward sipped and watered wine,
as if we couldn't smell.
The quartermaster shaded cards,
the carpenter shaved dice,

the bursar misreported
in his ledger so precise.
There was an undercurrent
dragging us along,
though breezes blew,
our pennants flew,
and someone sang a song.

Sunrise of the second day
the clouds were bloody red,
the sky was greener than the sea,
it filled us all with dread.
We thought about Xavier,
never lost at sea,
never frightened by a storm,
such calm serenity.
Where there were troubled Christians
on some island in the night,
Xavier could find them,
something steered him right.
We asked, "What is your secret?"
He would only smile and say,
"Jesus is our compass,
Jesus is the way."

I know you must have heard some tales
of great typhoons at sea,
with every sailor thinking
this is punishment for me.
The ocean turns to mountains
and the mountains rush head on,

and each wave takes another man,
another shipmate gone.
Without a single sail aloft,
the wind snaps off the mast,
the rigging carries off more men
in the net of sin they've cast.
And then what we throw overboard,
what promises we make,
what desperate prayers,
"Xavier, I every lust forsake,
and every coin I'll give away,
with God, I will abide!"
A vision or a shaft of light,
the storm, at last, subsides.

That was not our experience.
Our storm was even worse.
Every single one of us
bore the selfsame curse:
We were not worthy of a storm.
We were such little men.
As mighty as that great typhoon
is what we should have been.
As faithful as Xavier
is what we ought to be,
Christianizing all the world
across God's every sea.

You see that we survived the storm.
Our beards, our hair turned white.
By day, we coast to villages.

We tell our tale by night.
We win another soul for Christ,
sometimes, two or three.
We make our way around the world.
We are not lost at sea.

Luis Camoes

1561, Saint Francis Xavier appears to Luis Vaz de
Camoes, jailed in Goa, and inspires him to complete
The Lusiads.

To convey to him in his dreams which port
Would offer the tranquility he sought.
   Camoes, *The Lusiads,* Canto Two, 56

My spirit sleeps through storm or quake,
or wakes to hear a psalm, a prayer,
the silence of your pen.
Your sleep is disturbed; your soul
  is disturbed.
I am like you. You've lost an eye,
you've lost your youth. Never mind;
it isn't what you lose, it's what you find.
Here is a sojourn of solitude,
locked in a sobering cell. Here you can do
what you say you can do, the thing that you
  do well.
Write when you awake. There is need
  of poetry.

Inspire your fledgling King with inspired
    Histories.
Praise the Portuguese to the gods;
praise God to the Portuguese !

Death of Mansilhas

1565, Cochin, India, Francis Mansilhas is dying.
The spirit of Francis Xavier attends him.

Keep me constantly informed about yourself and the
Christians, and hasten along with the building of the
church; and let me know when it has been completed.
    Xavier to Mansilhas, June 1544

Francis, why are you sorry?
Why are you praying for mercy,
forgiveness? Jesus loves you.
You have done well.
Let me tell you something.
You know that men called you
"Francis the Lesser"?
That is because I was The Great,
the great Disaster.
You never harmed anyone.
And you endured – everything –
poverty, misery, loneliness.
The world is full of sophisticated priests.
Heaven wants a simple one.
Thank you, beloved friend,
for coming with me to India.

I never deserved such devotion.
Come with me, now,
to your brothers in Heaven.
We have missed you.
I have no further tasks for you,
only rest and comfort and peace,
and the love of your brothers and parishioners.
Come, you have done enough.

Xavier's Chapel, Goa India

Followers Crucified

1597, in Nagasaki, six Franciscans, three Jesuits,
and seventeen Japanese Christians are crucified.

In these regions, as in many others, great services
frequently fail to be rendered to God our Lord because
of the unfortunate rivalries that exist between different
parties . . .
Xavier to King John III of Portugal, 1548

Here is death worse than war,
Franciscans dying far from Spain,
Portuguese Jesuits, death and pain.
Europeans, Japanese,
hanging from these Roman trees.
Twenty-six crosses on a hill,
Christians, children, dying still,
praying to the Savior, Come
take my soul, make me numb.
When we sought to win War Lords,
did we reckon on their swords?
What part our divisions played?
Which insinuations made it expedient
to kill the first fruits of Japan?
Too late now to be undone.
Too soon rising with the sun
to other islands,
where blossoms don't fade,
and silks don't bleed,
and the faithful don't hang
like so many kites in the wind.

Celestial Observations

1606, Sabatino de Ursis, S.J., astronomer,
reaches the Imperial Court of China.

As to the Western doctrine which exalts the Lord
of Heaven, it is opposed to our traditional teaching.
It is solely because its apostles have a thorough
knowledge of mathematical sciences that they
are employed by the state. Be careful to
keep this in mind.
           Chinese Emperor K'ang Hsi

Sleep, Sabatino, rest.
I am not Father Ricci.
You will meet him tomorrow.
I am Francis Xavier. I am a dream.
You read my letters from Japan
concerning the Chinese religions.
You are anxious to know about their calendar,
their concept of the physical heavens.
You are eager to begin.
I will give you an orientation
as you rest from your journey.

It is the Chinese year 4,304.
It is a year of the Horse.
It is a Bing Wu year in the 60-year cycle.

These years are lunar,
and consist of 12 or 13 moons.
But the formula needs adjustment.
The New Year recedes into Winter,

and the Emperor loses face.
Regulate their lunar calendar
and your reputation will be secure.

Bing is the third of the Ten Celestial Stems.
Wu is the seventh of the Twelve Earthly
    Branches.
The years are named by their pairings,
six times through the Stems and
five times through the Branches
until the cycle begins again.
Our years march through decades
and centuries and millennia to Eternity,
while Chinese years revolve.
Chinese wish to live sixty years,
to see their cycle begin again.
Their cycle of years without end
supports their idea of reincarnation.

The day, you will learn,
is divided into twelve equal intervals
named for the birth-year animals
which reside on the 12 Earthly Branches.
The Rat, Ox, Tiger, Hare, Dragon, Snake,
Horse, Goat, Monkey, Cock, Dog, and Pig
constitute the Chinese zodiac.
The animals of the time and year of birth
determine one's horoscope.
Calendars and Almanacs
are widely consulted.
Astronomy serves Astrology.

Few seek knowledge,
all seek foreknowledge.

But these same animals are not the
    constellations,
except for the Ox, always so visible in
    the landscape.
In the Chinese heavens, the stars combine
    as temples,
gates, pagodas, bridges, roads and rivers.
There is a bow, a dipper, a tiger's tail,
clutter in the celestial map.
The Chinese will not soon forego their heaven
for a Greco-Roman replacement.
Find your operative stars in their constellations.
You will know more than one Heaven.

Language will not be impossible.
Father Ricci is a gifted linguist,
and will teach you easily. This time,
you will learn to read and write
before you learn to speak.
There are thousands of characters
but only a few hundred components,
and even fewer sounds.
The language is visual, evocative, but not
    not precise,
perfect for Poetry, clumsy for Science.
But Chinese writing is art itself,
ultimately a labor of love.

Chinese compute small numbers by fives,
great numbers by ten thousands,
but, for its utility, they will adopt
your mathematical notation.

And many will adopt our true God,
His Son, and the hope of life eternal.
They will repent their sins, and live
   good lives.
But they will not altogether forsake
the ghosts of their ancestors
or the folk-tale gods of their childhood.
Let God be the judge of their beliefs.

Do not expect to return to Rome.
Embrace this work. Live your Faith.
We will meet again, in Heaven.

A Martyred Child

1609, Nagasaki, the son of a Christian martyr
is beheaded.

The leaping soul slips its body's prison
To claim the greater prize of the arisen.
  Camoes, *The Lusiads,* Canto Ten, 31

After the groans and sobs and retching,
a deadly silence descends.
Three bodies lie quartered.
It is time for the youngest to die.

Pedrico is five, son of Hattori Juan,
the Minister of Mercies, first to die.
Pedrico is a Christian,
baptized by Father Ferraro.
Ferraro is present, but bound and beaten;
these executions are for his instruction.

Two soldiers lead Pedrico
onto the field and release him.
The executioner advances from behind.
Of his own accord, the boy continues further,
strips to his waist and kneels down in the gore
that was, moments ago, his father.
The executioner staggers.
He cannot follow to that bloody spot.
He returns, sickened, to his ranks.

An order is shouted,
and another advances with his sword.
But the boy has begun to pray;
his hands are clasped,
his eyes are raised to heaven.
Already missing his father,
he calls to the soldier to hurry.
And this soldier falters,
and despite shouts and curses,
he drops his sword,
and goes reeling off the field.

A third soldier, a Korean, is given the order.
A stranger to mercy, but certain of his
   punishments,
he will not disobey. He advances quickly.

Oh Mighty God, transport me to this field,
and let my corpse become a human shield,
to stop this charging soldier in his path,
and demonstrate, once more, your
   righteous wrath,
and shock them with the horror of their sin !
Oh let me be your miracle again !
I cannot move – Oh Christ !
Why must this be?
The field begins to spin,
and though I already see this boy
ascending to the arms of Christ,
this soldier gibbering his way to Hell,
this place, Nagasaki, exploding
from the face of the earth –
I am not reconciled.
I am not strong.
And the rising sword flashes
at the instant of its descent,
and my spirit faints away.

Xavier's Arm Removed

1614, by order of the General of the Society of Jesus,
Francis Xavier's right arm is removed.
His shoulder is sent to Macao, his upper arm is
divided and sent to colleges in Malacca and Cochin.
His forearm and hand is sent to the Church of Gesu in
Rome -- where it signs his name.

Be assured, Doctor, that I am past pain.
Come closer. Have your men open the lid.
Lift me carefully, my neck is broken.
Be assured, Doctor, that I have revived
more than a few surgeons,
and held the hands of amputees.
If my arm alone could accomplish all
   I left undone,
I would have found a way to cut it loose.

There comes a time when the work of hands
does not suffice. We must have faith:
that a wound will heal, that a house
   will stand,
that a seed will grow; that some will tell
and some will hear, and some will believe;
that others will see and believe.
Remove the arm, Doctor.
Distribute portions as our General directs.
These bones will do more good
among people than in a crypt.
Those who believe in relics
believe in Christ, and so are blessed.

Those who question the power of relics
approach Christ.
And those who approach a step closer,
they are saved.

Saint Xavier

1622, Xavier is canonized by Gregory XV

How much better to hold in memory
One whose deeds are worth eternal glory.
 Camoes, *The Lusiads,* Canto Two, 113

I petitioned my family from school,
asking for letters of introduction
attesting to my aristocratic birth,
our place in society.

Knowing that I would use them
to incur further debt,
they did not reply.

Later, your Holy Father
pressed upon me his letter of appointment,
Papal Nuncio to the Portuguese Indies.
This I kept in my pocket,
and did not show anyone,
lest they ask for favors
I felt powerless to effect.

Brothers, forgive me.

Today, your Church proclaims

I am a Saint, forever.
The Pope declares what You ordain,
I will have opportunities to serve You still,
and power, according to men's faith,
to do your will.

Lord, redeem my troubled soul,
strengthen my spirit, accept my love,
make me wise, help me understand.

The Inquisition

1635, on the eve of an epidemic, from the tower of
Saint Catherine's, the Golden Bell tolls for another
execution.

Another need in India to protect the Christian life of
those who have been baptized into the faith is that your
Highness should order the establishment of
the Holy Inquisition.
Xavier to King John III of Portugal, 1545 and 1546

Adherence and obedience,
I never sought from such as these.
From their irreverent overlords,
to discipline the Portuguese,
I wrote the King. I prayed to God.
I died my death. Help never came.
But now my Inquisition comes
and builds a palace in my name.

Abysmal bell, that tolls the prisoner's
life away, but not his pain!
Accursed court, in search of weakness!
Twisted doctrine! Spreading stain!
Oh rotten ships, with instruments
of torture and a plague aboard!
Abhorrent hymns, proclaim these
horrors pleasing to the Lord!

My God does not mistake our prayers
nor misinterpret our intent,
but there were letters that I wrote,
letters I should not have sent,
beaches I should not have walked,
oceans I should not have sailed,
battles I should not have fought;
for worse than naught, I lived,
I failed.

Poems by Wu Li

Painter, Poet, Jesuit, Wu Li, Simon Xavier, S.J. (1632-1718) wrote the first Christian poetry in the Chinese language.

If what you teach is true,
why haven't we heard it from China?
          the Japanese to Xavier

Excerpts from *Heavenly Music Described*

Lamentation

None call the world wide;
six waters, three mountains,
divided fields.
Harvest the insects in a bowl.
Revert to every wrong.
Why? Secret sorrows.
Do not destroy life;
who can sustain life?
Do not find fault;
who is not guilty?
Who can understand?
Sword road, blood road,
neither living nor dead at peace.

Fat burns itself, fries itself.
Chinese and Tartars want alike,
caught in famine.
Go see the landlord,
argue for some way to eat.

Unavoidably, the poor
net birds, dig up rats.

The wealthy expel refugees.
They heed no warnings,
they can't be persuaded;
bottomless gluttons,
insatiable misers.

Above, the moon rounds the heavens.
Alas, nothing follows.
Stillness spreads, years lengthen,
their shape is indeterminable.
The sun pushes, the moon pulls.
Look away.
Be born, age, be sick, die.
Look within.
Smoke and clouds whirl and return.
Remember going and coming.
Wealth screens the palace.
Sampans cross the sea.

Music for the Mass

Begin in the key of A
the call to attend the Mass.
Perceive, perhaps, endlessness. Tremble.
Reach the altar as ceremonies begin.
Western music flows.
Emulate reverence.

Be humble, be respectful.
Gather, in my church, joy and faith.

Chanting The Rule

Who can leave the web of the world?
What sorrow to separate from people.
Who can evade life?
And how, without a net?
Rely on the ship's rigging.
Climb to heaven as easy as pointing.
Translate, publish, preach The Word.

The Chinese Oriole Rejoices

To my own Chinese last,
Holy Child, come, descend.
Teach living men to change,
to understand goodness, to extend mercy.
Let the Holy Mother, a virgin,
give birth in a stable.
Like a great choir, gather in Church.
Here is praise, the West is silent.
Save the lost and dying souls.
Sweep away the howling Devil.

Saint Francis Xavier

by Wu Yu Shan / Wu Li / Simon Xavier, S.J.
from *Thirty Hymns from Macau,* 1681

Words of praise to tell his story,
one who brought God greater glory,
forsaking wealth and ease of office
to share the gospel with the poor.

Appointed to secure the East,
confess the great and save the least,
he stood, the holy doctrine's pillar;
he followed Jesus down the shore.

A shepherd's endless watch to keep,
he crossed the jungles and the deep
enduring hardship with his sheep,
their dangers and their sorrows bore.

Out of India they flow,
his blessings from so long ago,
his spirit free to come and go
through China's closed forbidding door.

Enter saint, and point the way.
Bestow God's love and grace today.
Awake in us a flame, we pray,
for peace on earth forever more.

How can my poor words explain it ?
Do not oppose the Jesuits, truly
they are Asia's compassionate fathers.

Father Sandy holds a clinic
at Saint Xavier's on Sancian Island

The Age of Reason

1681, the Portuguese d'Almeida New Testament
is published – in Holland.
1682, Halley observes the comet.
1683, Doctor John Brown's illustrated *Treatise
of the Muscles* is published. Printing is forbidden
in the American colonies.
1684, Gottfried Leibniz invents Differential Calculus.
1685, Doctor Abercromby publishes *On Variation of
the Pulse*.
1686, Isaac Newton presents his *Mathematical
Principles & Natural Philosophy*.

This sphere I set before you represents
The whole created world, so you may see

Where you have been, and are, and wish to be.
  Camoes, *The Lusiads,* Canto Ten,79

The firmament is no less firm
because the world goes round the sun.
The word of God is not profaned
if spoken in another tongue.
The human heart is not defiled
because it serves to pump our blood.
Knowledge, Science won't explain
why God raised Adam from the mud.
Learn the riddle of the Sphinx,
explore another galaxy,
plumb the depths the ocean sinks;
you will not change man's destiny.
But, mortal, do not seek to learn
God's plan for Eternity.
For your part, save your soul !
Ask, Lord, what would you ask of me ?

Chinese and Malabar Rites

1740-58, Missionaries under Benedict XIV must take
the Oath rejecting and foreswearing the Chinese &
Malabar Rites.

In Malacca . . . my main occupation is . . . translating
the Latin prayers into a language which those in the
Macassars can understand.
Francis Xavier to the brothers in Europe, 1545

Ask those who are present: Do you believe in one true
God, almighty, eternal, immense, and infinitely wise?
Francis Xavier, Instructions for Catechists, 1545

Aramaic nurtured Him.
Hebrew schooled Him.
Latin condemned Him.
All understood Him,
each in their own tongue.
Being mortal and foreign,
we were not understood.
So we had to learn to teach
in tongues of Oriental speech.
We taught the children Adoration,
told the wise men of Creation,
showed the sinners their Salvation.
And in their language, not deceived,
they found His truth, and they believed.
Just how strong was their belief ?
Just sufficient for their grief.
Christianity was proscribed --
for their Faith ten thousands died.
Was faith, as they expressed it, True ?
They are with God, I swear to you.

All language becomes one.
I understand all; I speak none.
I hear this Oath, the undertones
convey resentment and mistrust.
I hear the Oriental Rites
continued, but not confessed.

The Church is divided, not blessed.
If I could, Holy Father, I would say:
Inquire. Reconsider. Pray.

Easter in Navarre

1763, Navarre Spain

That golden age of innocence, before
This age of iron experience and war.
  Camoes, *The Lusiads,* Canto Four, 98

In Spring, the shepherd boys take turns
to bring a lamb and ewe to graze
before the village church.
This pair is especially mild
or else they listen to the song.
It is a little weaver maid
singing the Ave Maria;
her lovely song transcends
a world of common cares.
And yet, it is the homily
the Padre gives in Basque
that resonates within;
not his simple sermon,
which all have heard before,
but my mother's tongue
which I have not forgotten.

It is the Easter season;
two girls and a boy receive

their First Communion.
Their mothers weep,
their fathers feel like weeping,
but not from religious ecstasy.
With adulthood comes
regrets and disappointments,
and the certain knowledge
that idyllic peace does not last.
Man and nature do their worst.
And only between tragedies
will they find such times as these.

Exiles in Wales

1773, Pope Clement XIV dissolved the Society of
Jesus.

"White Russia is now the most fortunate province
in our empire. Its youth are trained by the Jesuits."
                              Catherine the Great

1774, Xavier University in Wales

There, with a laden beak, the linnet pressed
Back with a gift of food to her dear nest.
    Camoes, *The Lusiads,* Canto Nine, 63

To my brothers in exile, assembled in Wales,
Rest, assured of God's blessing.
We have strived through all the world in
    our labors.

Know now that there is as much efficacy
    in prayer,
and that it is good to be gathered together
as first we were, a few friends,
praying to God, in the ruins of a church.

How it moved us to witness each other
surrender to His love, and arise to
    His purpose.
But, Soldiers, kneel down, it is time to pray.
It is time to study, time to write.

Write to your churches.
Encourage them!
Though failure haunts us,
though plague and slaughter follow
    in our wake,
they keep the Faith. Their souls rise up.
Their numbers grow. But they long for us.
Write! They will bear more fruit.

Likewise, Grow!
Sink roots, not in this remote place,
but in our Faith, and in our friends,
and in this time within His Spirit,
a holy, uplifting remembrance
when we once again disperse
to set the world ablaze.

Xavier's Cathedral, St. Petersburg, Russia

French Revolution

1793, Paris France, the College of Sainte-Barbe

And thus, when he was through,
The false god was worshipping the true.
 Camoes, *The Lusiads,* Canto Two, 12

My brothers in Christ and I lived here
hundreds of years ago.
And where Ignatius leads his friends,
I didn't want to go.
And all Favre exemplifies,
I didn't want to be.
They turned my very soul around.
Vive Fraternity !

I sold my horse to pay some debts.
I gave my cloak away.
I laid my sword in the Virgin's arms,
and found that I could pray.
I left my Chair for the Holy Land,
I was called across the sea,
a pilgrim, a servant.
Vive Liberty !

Professions, confessions,
I've heard from rich and poor.
The hopes and fears of all mankind
are as they were before.

And the souls of kings and fishermen
the Lord has saved through me
are worth no less or more than mine.
Vive Equality !

Jesuit Order Restored

1814, Pope Pius VII restores the Jesuit Order

". . . those closest to God will never be
lacking in some perfidious enemy."
  Camoes, *The Lusiads,* Canto One, 71

And so decisions are reversed,
the pendulum swings the other way,
and French intrigues are overturned;
we rise to serve another day.
But, Brothers, in our separate lives,
where every man must answer God,
it's usually the empty path
that follows where our Lord has trod.
So be more humble than we were,
and let the Lord redress old wrongs.
Consider how the world has changed,
and where each soldier best belongs.
And, where the heads of Orders meet,
stand to serve, do not compete.

Indiana Reconsidered

Saint Mary-of-the-Woods Indiana, 1842, the Sisters
of Providence have built a barn and filled it with their
first harvest. Anti-Catholics burned it in the night.
Sister Saint Francis Xavier fears divine retribution.

Reconsider Indiana !
Ere these ashes even cool,
comes another autumn morning,
come the children to the school.
And our neighbors come to ponder
what some ignorance has done.
And our barn was only lumber,
they will build another one.

Reconsider Indiana !
Though the storms rise in your breast
as you see our harvest smolder,
it is nothing. I attest
that here, in Indiana,
the good priest who brought me thence
has begun an institution
of enlightened reverence.
And Our Lady, loved and honored,
from atop its golden dome,
will smile down on Indiana
where her children find a home.

Xavier's Prayer

Prayer for the Propagation of the Faith
by Francis Xavier in Goa, 1548

Published in Spanish
by the Archbishop of Buenos Aires, 1847

Eternal God, creator of all things, remember
that You alone created the souls of
   the infidels,
making them in your image and likeness.
You watch, Father, in disappointment
as they fill the infernos.
Remember, Father, your Son, Jesus Christ,
who, spilling his blood so freely,
suffered for them.
You did not acknowledge, Father,
that he was your own Son and our Lord,
despised more than ever by the unfaithful.
As we reach out with the prayers & orations
of your chosen Saints, and of the Church,
the blessed spouse of your Son,
remember your mercy,
and forget their idolatry and unfaithfulness.
Make them know, too,
that You sent your Son, Jesus,
who is health and life and our resurrection,
by whom we are free and saved,
and to whom is the glory
through infinite centuries upon centuries.
                           Amen.

Francesca Cabrini

1857, Saint Angelo, Lombardy, Italy

We do not expect this voyage to be
as smooth and as beautiful as the last.
Travels of Mother Frances Xavier Cabrini
  New York to Nicaragua, October, 1891

Down comes Rosa to the stream,
holding Frances by the hand.
Frances holds a paper boat
destined for a foreign land.

Before the little boat can sail,
passengers are put on board,
violets that Frances picks
and dedicates to serve the Lord.

"Rosa, see, the first is you.
Children need good teachers there.
They've never heard the Gospels read
or any Christian songs or prayers.

"Xavier and I will go,
though none of us can speak Chinese,
and though he's old and I'm still small,
God can make us missionaries.

"Pray, help us find that distant shore,
and pentecostal tongues to speak,
and Chinese converts, Chinese friends,
to feed their poor and help their weak.

"Lord, who saved Xavier
incorrupt through ages past,
bring him to his feet again,
send him to Cathay at last."

After this prodigious prayer,
Frances sails her little boat.
It dips and bobs and whirls
into the current. Off it floats.

And Rosa, knowing paper boats
will soak the water up and sink,
tries to coax Frances away
from disillusion at the brink.

But Frances can't be led away
until her boat sails out of sight,
her paper boat, which should have sunk,
which sails with me into the night.

Mother Frances Xavier Cabrini

14 November 1880, Codogno, Italy, the first Mass is
celebrated for the Missionary Sisters of the Sacred
Heart of Jesus. This night, Frances Xavier Cabrini
dreams she has received a letter.

They say we have brought them true progress.
We hope this will result in good to their souls.
Travels of Mother Cabrini, Granada, 1891

Dearest Sister,

May the love of our Lord Jesus
give you comfort & strength.

Francesca, though it is not in your mind
    to do so,
you must attend to influential people.
Set them a higher purpose.
Let them build the Church,
a home, a school, a clinic at a time.
To them, at first, you will appear
as your daughters seem to you,
appealing, moved by simple cares,
until, interrupted by telegrams,
scheduled a year ahead, bowed with age,
your responsibilities eclipse theirs,
and the world calls you Mother.

Loving Sister, you must attend
to Orders and Institutions,
to Charters and Appointments,
for these, in perpetuity, repopulate themselves,
rebuild the very stones and beams
which crumble and decay
for as long as there is human need.
Be their patron saint.

Loving Teacher, do not mourn for China.
Chinese will find you in America,
where their need will be great.

Do not mourn for orphans;
become a saint,
and for every homeless girl
you must now entrust to others,
generations of girls will find you in prayer.
You will be with them, to love them,
to bless them, to lead them to Christ.

Your unworthy brother,
Francis Xavier

A relic of Mother Cabrini is returned to Italy

Xavier's Poem

1952, James Brodrick, S.J. concludes his biography of
Saint Francis Xavier: "Finally, for the sake of
completeness, it may be as well to say that the beautiful
Spanish sonnet beginning, No me mueve, Senor, para
quererte, loosely Latinized in the familiar hymn,
O Deus, ego amo te, is definitely not the work of
Saint Francis Xavier, however much it may reflect his
spirit." And he quotes George Schurhammer, S.J.:
"The sonnet was written by an anonymous author in the
seventeenth century, long after the time of St. Xavier,
who, in any case, was no poet."

O Deus, ego amo te

translated by Gerard Manley Hopkins, S.J.

O GOD, I love thee, I love thee -
Not out of hope of heaven for me
Nor fearing not to love and be
In the everlasting burning.
Thou, thou, my Jesus, after me
Didst reach thine arms out dying,
For my sake sufferedst nails, and lance,
Mocked and marred countenance,
Sorrows passing number,
Sweat and care and cumber,
Yea and death, and this for me,
And thou couldst see me sinning:
Then I, why should not I love thee,
Jesu, so much in love with me?
Not for heaven's sake;

Not to be out of hell by loving thee;
Not for any gains I see;
But just the way that thou didst me
I do love and I will love thee;
What must I love thee, Lord, for then?
For being my king and God. Amen.

Basque Nationalism

In 1895, Sabino Arana formed the Basque Nationalist
Party and proposed a new flag.
Shortly thereafter, a new hymn was heard.

And many knights came flocking in their pride,
All ready to be martyred at his side.
  Camoes, *The Lusiads,* Canto Three, 23

Who is coming to steal the sheep ?
What is this angry watch you keep ?
Why do you fortify these walls ?
Far away, your Savior calls.

What if a new flag flies above
the re-united realm of old ?
What does a man still yearn to love
more than his home, more than gold ?

What if this sovereign realm contained
another field, another hill ?
How much fruit would an acre yield ?
How many souls to do God's will ?

Carry your flag beyond this place,
beyond the next, beyond the sea.
Trade it for the Cross of Christ !
Follow Him ! Come with me !

Obedience

1543, a first priority of the new Company of Jesus was
to establish seminaries and publish catechisms in
Germany. The Counter-Reformation was underway.

"And though this world with devils filled
should threaten to undo us,
we will not fear, for God hath willed
his Truth to triumph through us."
A Mighty Fortress is our God
Martin Luther, 1483-1546

Cordula Wohler, 1845-1916, daughter of an
Evangelical Lutheran minister, embraced Catholicism
and wrote devotional poetry.
This is her poem, *Sankt Ignatius und
Sankt Franz Xaver*.
from the German

See two saints depicted here, friends
about to part.
Loyola gives the order that will sorely
wound his heart:
"Go forth, through the world so wide,
across the land and sea,
and preach the Word of Christ and Cross
and Christianity!"

47

Xavier kneels and praises God. He hears
    Loyola say,
"Obedience is called the Son, the Son
    is yours today."
Loyola hears Xavier humbly reply:
"I'll be a faithful missionary, until the day
    I die."

Xavier sails and sails again. He walks
    a distant land.
He baptizes thousands with his weary
    pastor's hand.

On and on, beyond the dawn, the Word
    of God he teaches,
until the soul of India for Christ's Salvation
    reaches.

And all he did – it was so great, it was so
    swift and sudden,
that people knew Xavier could not be only
    human;
and what he wrote of what he saw, it was
    so compelling
that he began the ranks of foreign
    missionaries swelling.

But what sustained Xavier, inspired his
    benedictions?
What light glowed along the path, despite
    his own afflictions?
What holy strength to roam the world, and
    win for Christ its heathen?
What begins the miracle of the Easter season?
Obedience. Give God your love!
    It explains the story;
those who find Obedience find Eternal Glory.

And who defeats his flesh and blood, and
    loneliness, desire,
defeats the world, and mortal death, and
    Hell's eternal fire.
Whatsoever God commands is possible
    to bear.

God gives each of us a path, it could lead
   anywhere.

Follow God! Obey The Call! Never count
   the cost!
Obey the Lord and you are saved, yourself,
   and you are lost.

Cantique a Saint Francois Xavier

ad maiorem Dei gloriam
Liege, 1905, from the French

marciale
In love, at first, with glory among men,
haunted by dreams so vague, so grand,
God led you to his greater glory when
He called you forth to preach in heathen
   lands.
Refrain:
Ardent Xavier, heart still aflame,
lead us to live for The Faith as you do,
following Jesus Christ our Lord and Savior,
let us be helpful and humble and true,
let us be loving and giving and true.

The words of Christ, in languages "profane",
of love and hope – not savagery,
and acts of mercy, none of it in vain;

you saved their souls ! Oh Saint, you're
   saving me !
Refrain:

Beyond the dawn, more millions wear
   the Cross,
they die and live as Christians do.
But heaven waits, your brothers count
   their loss,
Xavier, the saints are calling you !
Refrain:

Like Jesus Christ, you bring the living light,
loving and kind in all you do.
The scorching paths of earth have cooled;
   it's night.
Xavier, we come in search of you.
Refrain:

Le Cannet, Chapelle Saint Sauveur

Republic Day

In 1541, on his 35th birthday, Father Francis Xavier,
the first Jesuit missionary, officially the Apostolic
Nuncio to India, sailed from Lisbon aboard the
flagship of the colonial governor. The youngest son
of Vasco da Gama was imprisoned on the voyage.
Eleven years later, Xavier died on Sancian Island,
exiled, marooned by the Commandant of Malacca,
this same Dom Alvaro d'Ataide da Gama.

Portugal, 5 October 1910, King Carlos and Prince Luis
have been assassinated. The palace has been shelled,
a Republic proclaimed, and the last King Manuel,
20 years old, escapes from Lisbon aboard his yacht.

"The man who is not cowed by abject fears,
though life be short, his fame survives the years."
  King Manuel the First to Vasco da Gama
    Camoes, *The Lusiads*, Canto Four, 78

Now the churches all stand empty
for the faithful line the quay.
Though church bells ring, they ring
the king to exile from today.
And a new republic rises,
and, already, factions start,
and there's gladness,
and there's madness,
there is sadness in your heart.

But you have another kingdom,
you have another king.
His empire is eternal,

and his Peace is everything.
And he gave his son to save you
from ambition and your pride.
He forgives you,
and he loves you,
and his doors are open wide.

The Lost Letter

Leipzig, 1927, en route, unannounced, to Xavier's
biographer, an old antiquarian dies, and this relic,
in Xavier's own hand, is lost.

Ceylon, 1544
To my Brothers in Christ,

I have walked a field of slaughter,
corpses roasting in the sun,
not a weapon, no defenses,
spared or rescued – not a one.
These were heathens we converted,
there are countless others too.
Though I know that we must save them,
it could kill them if we do.

A disregarded scarecrow,
lost in sorrow for lost lives,
I called for their defenders
and their children and their wives.
Through stinging tears, and trembling

53

with outrage and with grief,
I saw their souls go rising up;
I witnessed my belief.

Courage brothers, faith and courage,
preach The Word with all your heart !
Justice rules a field of glory
where the angels take our part.
Earth is not the Paradise.
Death is but an hour's sleep.
Love and Peace will reign forever,
if our Faith in Christ we keep.

On Opposite Islands

Sister Xavier Berkeley, Daughter of Charity, came to
China in 1890; Mother of the House of Mercy, she died
in 1944 on Chusan Island, at the age of 83.

Chusan China, 1933, on opposite islands

Everything belongs to God,
even on the Isle of Hell,
these hundreds of pagodas
where the bonzes with their idols dwell.

And everything belongs to God
on Sinkomen, across the way,
where nuns have brought the children
to celebrate a Holy Day.

They disembark, and two by two,

they come singing up the hill
in smocks of white with sashes blue;
their voices clear to Heaven trill.

And every one belongs to God.
Pilgrims with their loads of grief
trudge on up the hills of Hell,
and pay the price of their belief.

The children that they gave away,
now rejoice on Sinkomen.
Their parents pray for mercy still,
then, sadly, they descend again.

But everyone belongs to God,
and the Mother of all Mercies will
someday reunite us all
on an even higher hill.

Dominica, St. Sauveur Bay and Church

Spanish Civil War

Autumn 1936, Xavier Castle, Navarra, Spain

Viva Cristo Rey !   Viva Cristo Rey !
Shouts from the uprising in Pamplona, July 1936

Along the little Aragon, Miguel and Juan and I
chased the strays that crossed our boundaries
into our yards and pens.
Our father was always suing
someone for their forage and keep.
He won his suits at law, but no real
   compensation.
The courts confirmed his seigniorial rights,
but our neighbors had only those few sheep.

We always seemed to be at odds with our
   neighbors.

When I was ten, the forces of the late
   King Ferdinand,
under his Cardinal Ximenes, nearly leveled
   the castle,

and they filled up the moat,
and they revoked our feudal rights.

Later, my older brothers fought with the French
and the Navarrese separatists against Charles
the Fifth, the grandson of Ferdinand.
They were victorious,
capturing the citadel at Pamplona.

But, their canon nearly removed the legs
of my future Captain, Ignatius.
And the greater French forces were soon
    defeated.

The castle has been rebuilt, several times.
Now it is your school.
Here, you will learn political doctrine
and the tactics of mechanized warfare.

Loyalist, Nationalist, and ardently Catholic,
you already know your classmates,
like most of Navarra, at odds
with the rest of the Basque.

I have tried to suggest
that proceeding from this place
you may win campaigns, and still
not realize your ultimate objective.
Your Nationalists are already allied with
    evil regimes.

Already there have been atrocities
committed in the name of God.
There will be much to answer for.
Do what you must !

This, only, I ask of you,
while you are a guest in the home
    of my mother,
come into the chapel. Pray !

Japan Revisited

3 December 1952, in a suburb of Nagasaki,
on the 400th anniversary of his death,
Saint Francis Xavier's Church is rededicated.

Hear our prayer !   Hear our voice !
Hear our song ! We have come to rejoice.
Where the thousands died one day,
now the tens of thousands pray.
We have sorrowed. Today, we rejoice.

Though we mourn, though we die,
still we resurrect our steeple in the sky.
Where the atom split apart
and destruction stopped our heart,
we return, we rebuild, we reply:

Bless our church ! Let it stand !
Let its peace and beauty spread across
    the land !
If it ever falls again, let a hundred
    million men
build cathedrals without end !
Let the Love of God descend on Japan !

Portuguese India

December 1961, Indian troops occupy
Portuguese India

To what new catastrophes do you plan
To drag this kingdom and these people?
  Camoes, *The Lusiads,* Canto Four, 97

There is no golden treasure here,
save what you may hold in your heart.
These jewels adorning my casket
are glass replacements of glass
    replacements,
because the wrong beliefs persist.

And in the streets, no prize,
only the same commerce as before,

not especially profitable.
And in the offices, only Public Office,
with authority to preside over
public works and public debts.
You will not win your Freedom,
for you already know your burden,
only Self Determination,
however many tongues and creeds and clans
that Self of modern India may be.
At least it won't be the Portuguese presiding.
And so you come to take the cities,
as men do, to be important.

We could have traded and taught and
    ministered
and built without the rule of colonial empire,
if truly all we did was for God and for good.
The need to defend our interests implies
    otherwise.
Inevitably the buffalo would, someday,
flick the flies from its tail.

This age is ended, another begun,
political ages, in an ageless land.
The fields, still ruled by the sun.
Tigers reign in the mountain forests,
and crocodiles in the jungle rivers.
Ganesh abides in the ancient temples,
and elephants work to the old rhythms.
Great grandchildren ride the same trains.
Women still come to the wells.

Children gather grass and sticks.
Men tend their animals, and plow.
Tea and nuts are harvested in season
and carried down to the ports.
And the sun sets in the sea.

We leave behind our surnames,
some dances, stories and songs.
The churches of Goa and I remain.

Cultural Revolution

Cost what it may – to save one soul,
Death or a lifelong toil for Thee –
Gladly I offer all I can,
Lord, in Thy goodness, strengthen me.
      Francis Xavier Ford
    martyred Bishop of Canton

1969, San Chuan Island, The People's Republic
of China

The old men, the fishermen, remember
how, now and then, a passenger ship
would anchor off shore,
and its sailors would lower the boats
and row the passengers to the beach;
and these foreign devils,
woozy from the surf, and
overheated from too many clothes,
would pay to be carried or

pulled up the hill to my shrine.
They paid in a bewildering
variety of currencies,
each new specimen causing
speculation and haggling
for weeks afterwards in the market.
Most of the pilgrims were generous,
all of them harmless. They said
they came to honor a holy man
who died here four hundred years ago
while waiting for a smuggler
to take him to Canton.
The Portuguese had marooned him,
but other Portuguese had come back
and taken his body away.
And finally this church had been built
on the site, for the glory of their God.

They looked funny when they worshiped,
kneeling and standing and kneeling
    and sitting
and singing and sleeping and crossing
    themselves;
and then filing to the front, and
sticking out their tongue to receive
    a cracker.
But they were serious and pious about it,
and some would weep when leaving
    the shrine,
just a few hours after they had arrived.

And then the church would stand empty,
except for its caretaker, sometimes
for months at a time.
And then he was evicted,
and that was twenty years ago.
It is just as well that the young sailors,
advancing from the weather station,
are not bemused by any fond memories.
They chant as they come:
Down with antiquities!
Down with superstition!
Down with foreign interference!
But shouting less and less,
winded from the climb.
They pack together in front of the church
and kick open the door. It was not locked.
They knock over the pews
and hammer them with plaster statues.
They throw chunks of plaster
to break the windows,
especially the stained glass.
One sailor pisses on the alter, as did
   my acolytes
to their fathers' idols at Tuticorin.
Then they take the books outside,
   to burn them.
Had they looked, they would have seen
Bibles and hymnals and prayer books
in Chinese and Portuguese,
English and Spanish and French,

an elaborate Rosetta stone.
With the addition of desks,
this could have been a College
of Linguistics or Theology.

By now it is dark,
but their bonfire is a disappointment.
Burning books do not illuminate,
they just smolder; their silent echoes
are the scattered phosphors
glowing below in the South China Sea.
They leave quietly.

The party cadre is satisfied,
finally, he will have something to report.
But the sailors sense
that something was lost
and nothing was gained.
The old fishermen could tell them
(but no one ever asks),
from their own experiences
in Macao and Hong Kong,
that where antiquities are preserved
and church services are held,
and visitors are welcome,
they come, and spend money,
and do no harm.
But now, who will ever come
to see a desecrated church?

Xavier's Church on Sancian Island

All that Remains

January 1975, in Goa, India, there is another exposition
of the remains of Saint Francis Xavier. It is not the last.

Wherever a people place their trust,
The little they rely on turns to dust.
Camoes, *The Lusiads*, Canto One, 105

"I have yet many things to say unto you,
but ye cannot bear them now."
Christ to his Disciples, John 16:12

I am carried in a great procession
through bright daylight
from the Basilica Bom Jesus
to Saint Catherine's, the Holy See.

A million pilgrims line the way.
They throw flowers.

Choirs of children sing.
One balcony has collapsed,
resulting in tragedy.

The ardor of the crowd increases.
Many, though devout, are not Christian;
my mummy is another idol,
venerated for their preservation.

Christians seek their legendary relic,
watch for a sign or a miracle.
See him, touch him, kiss him,
and be saved, be happy, be healed.
Come then, and kiss me.
I will bear your love and your sorrows
to our Savior, Jesus.

But look, see how I crumble.
And when you leave this place
to return to your homes,
know that I have done the same.

I am not in this body, in this casket,
not in these holy shrines.
I am as I wish to be.
I am at peace.

Where will you find me?
Long ago, I wrote you letters.
Read them. Write to me.
I love you. I hear your prayers.

The Poems

The Pictures

Dedication:

To their translators
and biographers, especially,
Landeg White,
M. L. H., James Brodrick, S.J.,
M. Joseph Costelloe, S.J.,
Georg Schurhammer, S.J.,
Clementine de la Corbiniere,
Elisabete Ferreira Sakai, and
Sisters Ursula Infante and
Philippa Provenzano, M.S.C.

Special Acknowledgement

I would like to thank The Oxford University Press for
permission to use couplets from their 1997 edition of
The Lusiads to introduce some of the poems in this
book. I can find no better way to evoke
The Age of Discovery.

The Lusiads is Luis Camoes' story of Vasco da Gama's
voyage to the Orient. Francis Xavier reached India
about fifty years after da Gama. Camoes would have
been writing *The Lusiads* in the Orient about ten years
after Xavier's death. It was published in 1572.

In the Oxford University Press, World's Classics
edition of 1997, translator (and scholar) Landeg White
retained the original structure of Camoes octaves
without trying to mimic the Portuguese internal rhymes.
Instead, he closes each octave with a rhyming couplet.

Made in the USA
Middletown, DE
31 August 2018